Michel van der Stel M.A.

Painfully Honest

© 2012

contact@michelvanderstel.com

Michel van der Stel M.A.   Painfully Honest

Contents

White space 4
Jesus Jerk 5
March 1989 7
March 1989 8
Shades of meaning 9
24 March 1998 10
York 11
To lose 15
List 17
18 April 2009 19
28 April 2009 21
On the day that Queen's Day has been cancelled
because of a failed attempt to attack the Queen 22
Grains of Sand 27
Unlocked 29
Bird 32
23 May 2009 33
24 May 2009 34
May June 1991 35
Surviving a 2 hr sleep Tuesday 39
To my Dear 41

On the day before my 41st birthday 43
8 June 1994 45
Ties & commitments 46
Riding shotgun in the night 47
FD musings 50
Long distance lost love call 52
Music in the Park 56
Parked 61
Hastings 63
July 1990 65
Easy 67
27 August 1991 69
6 September 1993 70
Moved 72
Still 73
On fellow humans & their behaviour 74
November 1989 76
I can't forget fifteen 77

White space January 1990

I stepped inside the room
And saw the rubbish lying
Over the chairs the table the cupboard floor
Collected paper piece of cloth
Tapes and books & teddy bears
An empty basket full hung standard
A board of chess painting half done
& brooding sea-elephants on the telly
the walls showed a similar disorderly view
photos of the dead & famous
& white space in between
I set down in the claret coloured easy chair
To rest my feet awhile &
To not upset the hospitality
My host was showing me
The room had a view of leafless trees &
Supermarket blocks of flats &
Dullish sky
My eyes returned to white space
My body felt the rubbish
When
I
Fell
ASleep

Michel van der Stel M.A.　　　　　　Painfully Honest

Jesus Jerk 15 February 1992

I like to jerk off
While watching
An electronic church
A preacher straight
From God
Hallelujah thank you Jesus
Healing hour
You'll be saved
My dick is getting harder
While a spectacled woman
With lilting lip &
No make up is
Climaxing in public
While all their hands are
Touching her
My hand touches
Pumped up penis
Pubic hair
Talk of sin damnation
Hell & Satan please
You upright preacher of the Word
Purity & righteousness
Oh make me come
Agh make me come
Heal some cancer patient
Crippled man or
Cursed Aids sufferer
Jesus dined with
Lepers
Use those hands
Get physical
Touch them
Touch them TOUCH

Michel van der Stel M.A.   Painfully Honest

Them –
 Oh make me
Make
It's getting harder
God
Good God
I burn in
Hell
Yes that feels good
Baby-preacher
Sex-tv

March 1989

To see some lovers' embrace sickens me,
As strayful fingers play with willed hair—
Perceive I warm-lipped kissing: stricken be
By brazen shaft of covet & despair
That presently these cheeks no heat can find
In bless'd proximity of thine: red-rosed.
Then do I curse these signs of love & mind
That knavish boy's beauty, in thee engrossed;
Then do I loathe I've lost love's labour's sweet,
And aching boils upon my heart I set.
Thus self-illed with perception and conceit,
I once more am made clear why we have met,
And self-transposed I your return await,
With Patience as the porter of my gate.

March 1989

Again with aching stomach filled with air,
Across the street I stood with bag & hope,
In expectation I was waiting there,
To catch but just a glimpse, an eye's quick grope.
Your gait an indecisive was, your eyes
A mixture had of sadness & delight,
Directed by two pulling dogs, our ties
Still proved too strong to stop at merely sight.
The two month absence was forgotten soon
As we embraced & kissed & touched once more
And Time did seem to melt the unseen moon
Into a constant mould of ne'er before
Felt unity, to share this with two hearts
Of mortal boy & girl, completing parts.
The secrecy was there before, the fun,
The warmth & honesty, pervading love
Of greater radiance than heaven's sun
Whereof the makers with deep draughts did prove.
Between us twain no jot was changed, except
That Love's firm knot through longing abstinence
An even tighter knot became, well kept
In heart by lodgers of love's residence.
But yet the world around did changes see
That turned high-yielding into unfertile soil:
Acorn grows oak in patient secrecy,
To thus escape destruction by turmoil.
Awaiting better times with constant mind
In faith that firmly leads to Rosalind.

Shades of meaning March 1990

The scratched & dead cheap pair of shades
Through which I view my world
At times organically transform
Into explicit flesh –
Integral parts of my face
They must their time abide there
To take off seems to mutilate
A precious balanced wholeness
Akin to lipo suction of the nose
The blotting out of eyes
Or seaming up of lips –
Disturbance of essentials
The withered plastic of new flesh
Shows throbbing veins just visible
A needle prick will hurt the nerves
A blow will break the spectre-bones
They've so become a part of me
I'm no longer amazed
And then
It's time
To take them off

24 March 1998

When Hapgood coined the
Earth's shifting crust phrase
Back in the late 50s
Could he have had the
Slightest inkling that two score
Minus one year later
Someone on another continent
Would be fanatically joyous
To find that this theory would
Seem to fit seamlessy with
His own unpublished ideas
Coming from a line of seamen
Dating back before Hapgood's
Book

York, 6 April 2009

On board the
Pride of Rotterdam
The Europoort
Embarked &
Cabined
The pre
Easter
Holidays
Have begun &
I will
Initiate
It
With a Guinness
Or three
We enjoy an
Evening meal
Sprinkled over with
Small talk
Students walking
Past and
Past again
Dancing
And then
Morning comes
I'm home
Again
Welcome back
Is screamed by
All things
English
A recognition
Beyond repair
Hello Hull

Michel van der Stel M.A.　　　　　　　Painfully Honest

Hello Yorkshire
The rows and
Rows of hedges
Dual carriageways
The A1079
Past the exit
For
Nunburnholme
The sun is touching
Me
Through the
Glass windows
Of the coach
With sign
Saying that
Seat belts must be worn
At all times
B&Bs along the
Road
And road signs
Warn for crossing
Deer
The morning York
Brings the
National Railway Museum
Where I am awed
By train saloons
Of royalty
Among which
The Duke of Sutherland's
Self-contained
Coal furnaced 2818 Great Western
Fin de siecle 19C
Bolted
Edward VII's

Bathroomed
Bathtubbed saloon
 And the saloon of
Queen Victoria
Who handpicked the
Bird's eye maple and a mixture of red,
White and blue and gold silk materials
My kids would have loved to see
The trains & all their
Pump and circumstance &
The pride in heritage
Afternoon York
Is for
The Shambles &
Cream teas
In a quaint and
Rustic tearoom
Is for the
York Minster
Where the Quarter Jacks
Hammer
Where Jeremy
Muldowney
Passionately preaches
The gospel of Cathedrals
Glass-stained windows
Choirboys playing football
Inside
Market scenes inside
Sings about the
Quire
In old Yorvik
Where the Foss
Meanders
Quietly

Michel van der Stel M.A.   Painfully Honest

I have a
Constant
Incessant smile

Michel van der Stel M.A.　　　　　　Painfully Honest

To lose 13 April 2009

My Oxford dictionary
Tenth edition
Completely revised
2001
Has on page 841
Between
Los Angeleno
And losing battle
The words
Lose /luːz/
&
Loser
From the
Old English
Losian
Which means to
Perish or
Destroy
And that's my
Angle
I have been
Destroyed
I have perished
A living dead
That fuels
On
Drink
To make it
Through the
Quiet of a
Sunday evening
Hee loser!
Wash your

Michel van der Stel M.A.   Painfully Honest

Face
You
Lost
The game
You played
Gambled
Doubled, tripled
The stakes
&
Lost

Michel van der Stel M.A. Painfully Honest

List 17 April 2009

I am compiling a
Thank you list for
My upcoming
Publication &
You are not
On my list
For you have
Never motivated
Inspired
Stimulated
Me
You buy me
Exquisite fine
Food &
Oranges &
Cakes that
We eat
With our
Cups of coffee
And I translate
These gestures
As I love you
And I have
Respect for
How you live
Your life
My son
Yet never a
Question asked
About who I am
Or
How I feel
Awkward

Michel van der Stel M.A.   Painfully Honest

Embarrassing
Silences
Occur
So little
In common
Not on
My list

Michel van der Stel M.A.   Painfully Honest

18 April 2009

Yesterday my three
Had a local charity sponsor
Run
So
Of
Course
I had to be present
To support
In my car
Turn the key
No ignition
I'm going to miss the whole thing
Disappointment
Me the three
Called the Hyundai
24 hr repair service
Flat battery could you believe it
Left a tiny light on for two
Days
And the battery dies on me
Luckily
An easy fix
Missed the start
But
Was there for the last full
Forty minutes
Even ran a couple of rounds
With Timothy my sweet
Timothy
Took pics
Told them how proud I was of them
Held them
Got kissed

Michel van der Stel M.A. Painfully Honest

Emotions
Ran in me
As fast as the three
Did their rounds
Now that's a way to
Spend a Friday evening

28 April 2009

An apple
A bottle
A book
Another bottle
Of port
In my bag
6 garden plants
In the other
Rain
Gently falls
Down
I have just seen
My baby
Drank cappuccino
In the Golden Tulip Hotel
Overlooking the sluice
I didn't see the
Sluice
Cause I only
Eyed my
Baby

Michel van der Stel M.A.   Painfully Honest

On the day that Queen's Day has been cancelled because of a failed attempt to attack the Queen 30 April 2009

Queen's Day in the
Netherlands
Even the sun has an
Orange shine today
The country's come
To a standstill
I have my orange
National football jersey
On
Replica of the golden
Era – the 70s-
In front of City Hall
To have my
Traditional oranje bitter
Orange gin
The merchant mentality
Is what really makes
This day
Buying and selling the old
Stuff from the attics
While enjoying Surinamese
Food & a
Fernandes
The old decorated
Once fierce
Now feeble
Soldiers & their
WAGs are
Waiting for the doors
To be opened for them
There's about 6 dozen

Michel van der Stel M.A.   Painfully Honest

Of them
Barets
Big hats
And a strong
Sense of pride
As smiles on their faces
Almost eleven in the am
I am refused entry
By invitation only
As
The new
Double passported
Dutch Moroccan
Mayor
Has upped security
The scared chicken
Whom I have caught
Making basic Dutch
Grammatical mistakes
So now I'm
Browsing
For the scrappiest
Items on sale
For years the
City Hall Square
Where all the pubs are
Had a reputation
For growing ugly &
Violent
At around 6 pm
Each year
"No son
Those are dictionaries
They're not for you-"
Everything imaginable

Michel van der Stel M.A.   Painfully Honest

Is being sold
50ct hugs
Lots of clothes
Old sewing machines
Furniture
Russian uniforms
Ceiling systems
Gas ovens
Panties
Of course
I'm not only looking
At all the crap
That actually should all
Be thrown away in a
Landfill
Or better still burnt so
Nobody can ever use it
Again
Ever
But more so
I'm looking at the two sets
Of people
The sellers and the non-sellers
The latter which can
Be divided in two again
The buyers and the
Non-buyers who are just
Lookers on to the annual
Spectacle that
Never gets tiring
Wooden backscratchers
Bicycle saddles
Old records that
My parents had at home
On the

Michel van der Stel M.A. — Painfully Honest

Nieuwe Binnenweg
Where there's a
Real party holiday
Atmosphere
Two girls dancing to the
Mash potato
I walk into to the
Paradise church
And sit awhile
Contemplating all my sins
The heavily statued
Centre piece
With a victorious
And beaming Christ
It's not a pretty
Church
Has an office feel to it
An argument between
Seller and buyer
About the price
No doubt
An abseiling
Track is
Being set up
In the middle
Of the street
To the Oude
Binnenweg now
Where
The buttplug gnome
Greets us
On the
Coolsingel
I see
A cute tiny

Michel van der Stel M.A.   Painfully Honest

Orange bikini
That my sweetie
Would look
Sexy in
I bike home
Before the crowds
Come
And catch the
Flies that hitch
A free ride
There's a ladybug
On my crotch
Enjoying the soft
Fabric of my pants
And then I'm
Home

Grains of Sand 1 May 2009

Dig dig dig
Three newly bought spades and an old bucket
"Dad we found a treasure"
Electric wire and a shell or two
Building castles in the sand
The beach the waves
Elementary
Basic fun
In the sun
Strawberries & toast
On the boulevard
Running in their underwears
And a thick layer
Of sunscreen Walnut oil 30
I've taken tons of
Photographs
Dig dig dig
This afternoon's sole
Purpose
Ice creams later
Sand in ears
Between toes
On scalps
In belly-buttons
Timothy & Sebastian
Find
A 7 inch black
Metal
Spring
And dump it in
The bin
Tim comes running
Towards me

And tells me he needs to pee
 As a good dad I tell him
To just go pee
In the sea
He's six
And doesn't question me
So off he goes
Towards the sea
All the grains of
Sand
That we take with
Us
From the beach
Into the car
In our hair
In our home
Are little
Grains of
Happiness
Never to be
Taken from
The four of
Us

Unlocked 12 May 2009

Hope is the
Fuel that
Feeds the flame
So I'mme
Keep on
Hoping that
She will come
Tonight
Like I do every night
I'mme
Keeping hope
Alive
Hope is where
The heart is
Hope is more
Than a small
Town in a
Big state
She makes me
[so many things]
So I keep the
Front door
Unlocked
Tonight
Oh please do
Come
Oh please do come
My sweet
Beauty
My big
Love
Sweet angel
Mother

Lover
You
I need you
Daily
To have &
To hold
Me
Tightly
To look into
My eyes
And tell me
You'll not let me
Go
To look Truth into
His eyes
[Truth is a minor
God son of a
Major Goddess
Most probably
Venus]
And obey his
Rules
Be true
To thine own
Self
And so
To
Me
Or
To
Us
I love
Us
My front door
Is unlocked for

Michel van der Stel M.A. Painfully Honest

You
As
Is
My heart
Tonight
And every
Night to come

Bird 16 May 2009

This morning
Lazily in bed
Sebastian crept in
Beside me
Well half on me
Smile on my face
I asked him what
He would want to
Be later
He answered
That he wanted to
Be a
Bird
So that he could
Fly
To me
Always

23 May 2009

I've seen the
Evening
Shift into
Night
In the presence
Of beauty
My sweet
Young love

24 May 2009

Scheveningen beach
Again
Packed
The big
Brown bag
Full of everything
We need
Food drink
Sweets
Cakes
Towels & a
Tent
Buckets
Spades
A ball
Time does not
Exist
Temporarily
At least

Michel van der Stel M.A.   Painfully Honest

May June 1991

They sure could need new Noahs there
In cyclone-battered Bangladesh
Before the waters came
Running water cold & warm
For dishes showers or washing-
Machines
The choppers of the West pour down
Aid in boxes wooden boxes
That splinter on impact with
The surface muddy surface
Where clusters of people have
Their roots ankle & knee
Deep in the water
Neptune's will
Captured by the cameras of
BBC & CNN & other letters three
Making us donate still further parts
Of chip-chip-chipped off
Consciences
Where the irregular beating of
The President & this just in
Are intersparsed with Campari
Supper-cookers & hotels
Before the waters came
The fields where rice-seeds
Were planted were flooded by
More minor hands
& the right shoulder of
All-India never made
Bold lines of Western print
With the coming of each
Fresh cyclone
The value of Bangladesh

Dhakka
Relevant news
Fades
To a rare spot
On a news show late
& the middle pages
Paper pages of
The morning
Where this hour
The news is of
Another tribe
Where the water has come
The blood &
Perspiration
Counterweights for
Autonomy
Democracy
Free press
Haha
Fooled again
A proud nation nay people
Battered with words
Poison gas &
"Real live ammo"
To again fade in
The big back of minds
The Universal back of mind
Controlled by...
Where Kirkurk &
Sounds sharing samelike
Strength
Mosul
Sulamanya
Diyabakir
Are bastions

Michel van der Stel M.A.　　　　　Painfully Honest

Of a five-fold suppression
Where 1949 and later
71 are numbers sacred
Held in high esteem
Although many old men &
Women way past 71 will
Never see their universal right
When words are followed up
By inadequate action
Not to go against the superpowers'
Grain
And children dying refugees
With diarrhoea
Mystery illnesses &
Cholera
Before the waters come
Old Barzani
Reindeers &
Snow that varies 16
Times
Pure white dirty white
Gray powder strong
Iced etc perhaps
Scooters stripe the
Scenery &
Fire's made the
Natural way no
Campinggaz
In Northern Scandanavia
The Samis live & die & live
& speak their language
Swedes and Norwegians
Finns to name a few
So keen on drawing lines
On maps

Michel van der Stel M.A.　　　　　　　Painfully Honest

The bigger chunk is mine
The frozen water melts
In cans in Sami camps
I leave my seat
I turn the tap
Pour the boiled water
On the bag of cylon tea
I tasted snow
A rare small treat
Where now the grass seeds grow

Surviving a 2 hr sleep Tuesday night 3 June 2009

Stage 1
Getting out of bed

Stage 2
Checking myself in the mirror and
Deciding to skip the morning
Shower
Thereby adding another 15 min
Resting time

Stage 3
Trying to keep
Balanced on my
Two
Feet
Whilst doing my morning
Meditation

Stage 4
Brewing coffee
Ahhh
Coffee

Stage 5
Is climbing from
Hr to hr
As if they were
Alpine Mountain tops
And I a
Mountaineer
The bike ride over to
Work went surprisingly
Smoothly

Stage 6
Double espresso from
The employees' staff room
EspressoEspresso

Stage….
Ahhhh, too tired already
To keep on
Counting the
Stages
This is what they
Mean when they
Say
Death warmed up
Now I get it
Given the chance
I'd do it all again
And give up a
Night's rest
To create this
Piece of instalment
Art
Called loving her
Caressing her
Hr upon hr

To my Dear 6 June 2009

The prospect of a better World
Is what I see
Brought to us by the daring &
The brave
Cowards achieve naught
The outspoken become the strong
Not the other way around
Tell me without
Much ado
How you see the world
Are you inspired to
Soar up high
Upon wings of passion
And possibility?
Can you do a
Barry Obama
In the midst
Of potential
Adversity
And make em
Sway your way?
Pick your
Colour
Pick red
Leave the yellow
Be outspoken
Be bold &
Daring
Claim your
World
Take my passion
And all my
Possibility

Michel van der Stel M.A. — Painfully Honest

And swing with
Me on
Frankie's voice
Therein lies your
Prospect of a
Better world
My dear

On the day before my 41st birthday 6 June 2009

I have my
Focus
Fixed on the
Future
Steadfast
For
I know what I want out of life
I'll be old enough
Tomorrow to
Have made all my
Realisations into
Strong & clear
Directives
I'll be
Pursuing them
Relentlessly
Like a Super Croc
Snapping my jaws
Tightly around
My preys
I need to
Feed
My desires
Fill the
Cup to the Brim
And drink
The mead
God like
On my own
Olympian mount
I have
My eyes fixed
On

Michel van der Stel M.A. Painfully Honest

The ones that
Bring me joy
My lady from the
Sea
Is whom I
See
The three
By my side
Who ride with me
For all eternity
I know what I
Feel
No room for doubt
I'm old enough
Now
Made d o u b t
Into u do 't
And used the spare
b
To brush aside the
Arguments that do not fit
Brush away the cobwebs old
That obstruct my
Vision
I look at myself
(Thank you Heep) &
I look at you
And I like it all

8 June 1994

The indolence
I've experienced
During these last few days
Now
Has come &
Hung itself like
A kingly cloak
Around my shoulders
Heavy like a
Second skin
The passive pastime
Of the telly
Is salvation for
45 minutes a day
Of which I dread
The last few minutes
For what then
I masturbate with
Excitement
I play I read
I listen to music
All without passion
Languorous

Ties & commitments 13 June 2009

I cry
My tiny tears
& release
My sadness
Every so many
Days
That way
I worry about my
Three
I miss my sweet
Girl
It's getting so much
Harder as weeks
Go by to say
Bye bye to her & let
Her go
Release her
For she is my joybringer
And I want to
Perpetuate that
State of joy
For as long as
Possible
But I'm
Limited by the
Clock & by her
Personal circumstances
She is not a free
Agent
She is governed by
Ties & commitments

Riding shotgun in the night 20 June 2009

The local musicians'
Joint in
Old Gin Town
Is far from
Packed
Located on an
Industrial estate
Where dodgy car dealers
Do shady
Deals
The place
With its Mexican theme
Is perfectly situated
For music
Is not a clean
Business
It is messy
Greasy
Slick
Dark & moody
At the bar I
Order my one
& only beer for the
Night
As I am my designated
Driver
And enjoy it fully
Till last drop
Consumed outside in the
Friday evening setting
Sun
The battle of the bands
Commences & the few

Dozen
Music fans that are there are there
To support their brothers
Sisters neighbours friends grandchildren boyfriends
I seem to be the
Only one there
That has
Ulterior motives
For I am there
To enjoy the presence of my
Girl
I watch her arrive late
I shout in her ear
Something meaningless about the
Traffic or the band
Well the words themselves
Don't carry a lot of meaning
But the intention and the
Proximity of my head to her's
Pregnant with all sorts of
Overtones &
Undertones & middle tones
And feelings strong
I watch her interact
With her female friends
Who are in on all the
Secrecy that surrounds
Her
And receive the looks that are
Coming my way
With a proud smile
I watch her get
More drunk with
Every glass of port
Consumed

Michel van der Stel M.A.　　　　　Painfully Honest

And am told that
A woman drunk is an
 Angel in the sack
I watch her
She watches me
And so many thoughts &
Feelings are exchanged
In wordless silence
Speaking eyes
When the music stops
I drive off
Alone in my
Car
And dream that she will be there
With me
Riding shotgun
In the night

FD musings 21 June 2009

Father's Day
Is a Sunny one
This year
School made drawings
Of a giant
Daddy cake &
A steel brush
For a rusty chair
Best daddy in the
World mug
And hand printed
Tiles
Dated 2009
With the familiar
Corny Father's Day
Rhyme
That gets me all
Emotional nevertheless
Another good
Papa morning
And breakfast
Still needs to
Get started
The coffee goes in the
New mug
I shower with
My FD (Father's Day)
Shower gel
I start the
Car's engine
Turning the key that
Hangs from my new
FD

Michel van der Stel M.A.　　　　　Painfully Honest

Key hanger
A horse
We do something for me – visit
The first training of my
Favourite football
Team
Along with
15,000 other
Hopefuls
We do lunch
Toast & soup
And we go do something for them
Play in the
Speeldernis
Where I sit &
Write
On my sunny
Sunny
Father's Day
Now I am a
Rich man
And hum the
Famous bars
Softly dad a di did a da
Dom
Smiles are free
Today

Long distance lost love call 27 June 2009

I hope I'll ever
Be loved again
Like I was
Before
She tells me
On the
Phone
Calling long distance
Across the many
Time zones
Calling from
My
Yesterday
Referring clearly
To when I
Was her lover
In what now
Seems
A lifetime ago
But what has
In fact
Not even seen the
Moon
Wax & wane
Eleven times
Which makes me think that time indeed does fly
And has different
Speeds
For different
Episodes in my life
From the monumental to
The mere
Insignificant & mundane

Michel van der Stel M.A.   Painfully Honest

It ambles
Trots
Like a snail or a schoolboy with
His satchel… well you know
Wink homage salute
When I interject
That the boyfriend
She's currently living
With in
Oregon
And for whom
She moved almost
500 miles
Up North
The guy she
State-hopped for
Is madly in love
With her
She emphatically
Expresses her doubt
Repeatedly
I cannot reassure
Her that
She is worth loving
I get a series of fatal
& deadly
Whatevers
Tossed at me
To counter my remarks
I did love her
Once
Fully dedicated
A love song from
My
Yesterday

When I
Sang
Of Juniper
With
Donovan
Today is only
Yesterday's
Tomorrow
Uriah Heep
Proclaimed in the
70s
Funny thing these
Time zones
From East to West
It's back in time
So my Juniper
Is clearly in my
Past
Simultaneously
From West to East
Is moving forwards in
Time
So I am in her
Future
She asks about my
Current life
My love
My happiness &
I unashamedly
Tell her about
My sweet &
My love for her
Hoping at the
Same
Time

Michel van der Stel M.A.   Painfully Honest

That she'll
Again be
Loved
Like she was
Before

Music in the Park 28 June 2009

Took the midday
Train to
The Hague
Central Station
Train carried me
I carry my
Backpack and
Tons of memories
Of July 5th 2007
And days that
Followed
My experience
In love didn't kill
Me
Made me more
Convinced in what I
Want & what I
Do not
&
Now I'm here
Sunday afternoon
Past 3 pm
In a part of the park
That holds a pond
And a stage
On which the
Woodstreet Big Band
Will perform
Special guest the
Legendary
Rocker Andy Tielman
It's summer time
And a gentle breeze

Michel van der Stel M.A.　　　Painfully Honest

Is touching me
Its fingers
Through my hair
As I enjoy the
Beauty of all the
People – diverse
Around &
The occasional
Mellow dog
I sip my watered
Down orange juice
& my hard liquor
Flask is close at
Hand for
Later today
When I –
Like a dog –
Will mellow out
And lazy about on
This lovely
Sunday afternoon
Andy Rocker
Bearing his teeth
Continuously so
That it looks as
Though his teeth are a broad
White
Moustache
From where I'm
Sitting
Some
30 yards
Away
I have
Fun with what I see

Michel van der Stel M.A. Painfully Honest

An old man in
Tight shorts
Too short
Who is clumsily
Pulling up the
Zipper of his
Sports-jacket
The bandleader
Who picks up his
Sheet music and
Comes close to
Mooning us –
The audience
The one uptight
Dog in the
Park
A bitch
Is sitting and
Standing & turning
& digging &
Barking right in
Front
Of me
Barking her
Head off
Nervous wreck
Duetting with
The big band
Singer
Mariska
Who is doing
Her rendition of
Tragic Peggy
Lee's
Black Coffee

Dragonfly park
With lyrics
That can be
Described as
Interesting
Radar love
Weekend
I don't want to be
Your lover for the
Weekend
My dragonfly park
Neighbour of
Four seats away
Is doing his own
Performance
An entertainment
Story telling show – loud –
It's almost like
Being in love
Trumpets
Slide trombone
And the jazzy
Drums – Ludwig
True love
It's a wonder
Last song is
Cole Porter's
You'd be so nice
To come home
To
Listening to the
Lyrics & how
They're sung
I cannot but
Do so attentively

Michel van der Stel M.A. Painfully Honest

For I
Hear meaning in
Her words

Parked July 1991

The pulse of the city
Seems absent
Where the winds are
Free to roam
Play with grass & hills
Trees & kites &
Men
Where a girl without
Restraint
Pulls her shorts &
Strokes her butt
In the distance
Far & small
Some remnants of that
Pulse remain
Too strong a will to
Fade
Not even blur into the background
People wander
Through the park
An over-chubby man
With his shirt in hand
Shows tits
Some girls I know are jealous of
Where college boys gently
Steer their bikes
Their ATBs
Where madmen run &
Spit
Where fire-engine's rushing by
I eat
I sit
Madmen spit

Michel van der Stel M.A. Painfully Honest

Upon the park
Symbolic act
I ask
Malvolios moving on
Runners in the
City's unclean air
Strain their muscles
Burn their lungs
Where sex is nowhere to
Be found
This cornered speech
A cateract
A stream a torrent
Powerful
The city beats its beats
The cabs the buses
Underground
Where Richard
Drowned

Michel van der Stel M.A. Painfully Honest

Hastings July 1991

The battleground's as
Smeared with blood
As ever
A.D. 1991
Where ruins of a
Renowned castle
Charge £ 2.00
Or was it more
Fantasised over
For so long
A lustrum if not
More
Where 900 years of
Erosion
Have kept the smell alive
The blood won't clot
Puddles all around the field &
Clinging swords
Hacking swords
The hills are filled with
Children's cries
Now
Cries of joys contrasting death
I search death
The ancient ones
Yet find a boyish smile
I touch the grass
I bathe in it
My shirt is pierced
By arrows
William's men
Who won the day
My hands they

Michel van der Stel M.A. — Painfully Honest

Carry the day's
Stains of mud
Blackened blood
The child's baptised
In battleground
My face besmeared
With bloody mud
Muddy blood
It's William's tale

Michel van der Stel M.A. Painfully Honest

July 1990

Through the dirt-striped panes I see
Just how the sun's wavering rays
Are reflected on the tree's green leaves
I do not know the tree's name
Although I studied its movements bark and twigs
More often & oftentimes longer than
The times I made love these with myself included
What's the difference?
This study I am making involves not just this tree
Or its fellow companions that stand in
Our street. No it involves the neighbour who every
Tuesday sweeps his part of the street & hates to think
Of autumn coming soon the neighbour who sits inside all
Day keeping alive (& being kept alive by though but
Barely by) his vivid memories of WWII. His wife the
Leaves of grass our pet rabbit the aardvark the
Kangaroo the students in China the emu Romanian
Politicians Gorbachev. And our late 20th century legend
Who has already been compared to Moses and Jesus
Christ
Dear N.M.
They set you free some months ago
A long awaited victory
Looking strong & ill to me
I pray for you
Warrior
Symbol
Man
Not afraid of what's to come
Freedom & death
Death & freedom
So easily interchanged
We shall overcome

Michel van der Stel M.A.   Painfully Honest

We are not afraid
These words reverberate the hollow caves & cavities
Of unexplored…

Easy 7 July 2009

I miss you
The moment you
Walk out of my door
Every time a little more
I see the promise in your eyes
Feel all the kisses you plant on my cheeks
And on my lips and in
My neck
I feel your hand
Rubbing my belly
Still
Hours after you've
Gone
My love for you is
Strong
As is my
Faith in you
And a future for
Us
You talk about it
Every now and then
And that makes me
Smile even more
Your references to
A shared future
Seem to need
Confirmation
That I willingly
Give you
But then you're
Back in your present day
Reality
In between your two

Michel van der Stel M.A.   Painfully Honest

Different worlds
I miss
You
Every moment
That's not spent
With you
Time is precious
With you
Time is easy
With you
Oh God how I
Love being
With you
You make me
Whole
You nurse me
When I'm ill
You feed me
Quench my thirst
You love me
Most honestly
I want to
Be there for you
As a friend
To guard you from
The harshness of the
World
To comfort and
Console you &
To make you
Smile
I'll be there
My sweet –
Easy

Michel van der Stel M.A. Painfully Honest

27 August 1991

My life is marked by
Unimportant days
The ocean wherein
The rarer days
Swim freely
For all the ample
Space
That separates
Yet I cannot for
The life of me
Distinguish days
Of great
Importance
Unless tomorrow
Be such a
Day

6 September 1993

I cannot synchronise
My watch
At it
Although it happens
On a daily
Basis
The moment nay
Rather
The instance
When my idiom
My words
Blur into one
Big enormous word
Not to be pronounced
Of course
The inability to
Speech
Is like a punishment
Silence as the
Penance
As my hairy shirt
While the capacity to
Understand
A situation
Remains wholly intact
The tongue is out of
Order
I'm literally
Dumb-struck
And know no words
To match my thoughts
No single word can match
My lucid & coherent thoughts

Michel van der Stel M.A.   Painfully Honest

I know no
Words
Period
Now I could tell
You that this gigantic
Blurring is similar to
A topping of whipped cream on
A hot chocolate
Or to a particular
Cloud formation on a
September day
But I won't
Because it lacks
Precisely the
Essential part
The particle
The gravity of
The core
Namely that…

Moved October 1990

I have left my mark
Upon this World
I'm sure of it
I must have been eight years old
When I woke early
It was a Saturday
And autumn entered its fifth week
Or was it its sixth? Watercold
Anyway
The sun was lurking just above the horizon
I took one of my deepest breaths
Exhaled…
And left my soul on the icy pane
Through which I viewed the
World my world
I haven't moved on since

Still 2 October 1991

The seeds ejaculated
Ripples in the pool
The plants – dead
Still the capacity
To produce
The seeds take in the
Drops – swell
Prick their roots into
The rare desert sand
Moist – wet
Then buds more
Budding flowers
Multicoloured spectrum
Seed to seed
The drought-return
Away the array of
Techni-colour rainbows
Withering tombs
Containers of their
Former state of self
The cacti tower
High above
Selfishly
Phalli in a natural system
That poison the well
The desert people worship
Still

Michel van der Stel M.A. Painfully Honest

On fellow humans & their behaviour 21 October 1994

From the inability to conceive
An impression
Of expressions of feeling
In other fellow humans
I cannot distract/deduct
The total lack or
Absence of those feelings
Or the non-existence of
Expression
This reads like a dictum
To me now
A fault to easily made
An open door perhaps
From the poverty of
Contact
I build up myself
Like the British paper
Old established neutral
My sensors are on
The sonar's filtering
The sounds into classes
Intelligible / hardly so /
Trivial / senseless
And so I pick up
Threads loose ones
Of fellow humans
A train's a really nice
Place to monitor behaviour
A 30 min trip South
Through dull Dutch landscape
Is rich in gems & other
Precious stones
1 talk on work or school

Painfully Honest

3 reading a paper or book
7 staring out of the sand-
Tear stained windows
(This last category is as
We can see practised
The most yet needn't be
Less interesting than the
Above)
If a subject is a serious
Starer a real gazer
It makes an ideal subject
For study
The clothes the nose the
Hair the shoes maybe also
The luggage
Well you think of
Things to study when
You see somebody waiting
To be observed
Anyway I started out
By saying that
Impressions of
Expressions are not
Always made on me
And that one of the
Reasons for this is that
Maybe (for I'm not sure)
My skin's become too
Thick
At times
At places
At ease

November 1989

When most I long to lay me down abed
As when my world turns weary stale & gray
Remember I then every word was said
In comfort 'gainst despair so that I may
Continue still to labour for my end
That proves so constant clear here in my hand
Of greatness recognition's sword unbend
Inheritance by purest will so planned?
Contrasting answers here are yes & no
For understanding tends to mud at times
Accumulating all the pangs of woe
And louder than the loudest knell then chimes
Sweet yes I do for in forsaking thee
I lose my love my life praised poetry

I can't forget fifteen December 1990

The festive season
Looms over my dwelling
Where ribbons red &
Artificial snow
Fail to succeed in spreading
The warmth I know
A dying tree with lights &
Bells
Making times so merrily –
Oh peace on earth
Love & best wishes
The saviour on that day was born
They say
He is the light the way
And seems a lewd &
Clever trick for commercial
Enterprise to sell the goods
Unnecessary –
The snow keeps sticking to the
Panes & won't come off &
Melt dissolve in dew
For this too too sullied me
To enjoy the happy days to come
I can't forget fifteen

Printed in Great Britain
by Amazon